God's Holy House

Written by Amy Norris

Ilustrated by Alexis Olguin & Amy Norris

God's Holy House
is made in you and in me,
and all the parts
of your body
are very special
you see

19 Do you not know that your bodies are temples of the Holy Spirit, who is in you, whom you have received from God? You are not your own; 20 you were bought at a price. Therefore honor God with your bodies.

(1 Cor. 6:19-20)

When a good person gives in to the wicked, it's like dumping garbage in a stream of clear water.

(Proverbs 25:26)

Your eyes are
like windows
They were meant
to be clear
So you can see plainly
without confusion
or fear

Your body is Holy in
all of its places
For God is the keeper
of all of its spaces

23 May God himself, the God who makes everything holy and whole, make you holy and whole, put you together - spirit, soul, and body - and keep you fit for the coming of our Master, Jesus Christ.

(1 Thessalonians 5:23-28)

He covers you
and made you
just as you are
And you are
so beautiful
so precious by far

"... you are precious in my eyes ... and I love you."

Isaiah 43:4a (ESV)

Because He is such
a giver of life
He wants to protect
parts of you
meant to be OUT of SIGHT!

Parts under swimsuits
that you don't
want to share
Should be treated
with only
the greatest of care!

"See that you do not despise one of these little ones. For I tell you that their angels in heaven always see the face of my Father in heaven."

Matt. 18:10

Even if someone
you know
Or maybe someone
you trust
Tries touching
your bottom,
your privates,
your bust

REMEMBER
This is the truth
Don't be confused
from within
This is not your fault,
your shame or your sin

I am the Lord
and I know the ways of all
I know the good and bad
and I know whom I call

I am a God of light
Not a God of hidden things
I do not delight in secrets
or lies or sufferings

So if they say
it's our secret
and won't let you share
Don't listen to them
they are not playing fair

Love does not delight in evil but rejoices with the truth.

(1 Cor. 13:6)

I delight in
the truth
So do not be afraid
Do not keep quiet
This mess thats
been made

Pray to me and I will show you
the way that you should go
Who you should tell
and what they should know

I know what
is best
So trust me to
care and not
leave you suffering
alone in despair

Do not think of
the trouble
that the other is in
For it is MY
place to deal
with their heart
and their sin

Tell someone else
Teachers and Doctors
are best
Tell them right away
I'll take care of the rest

Written by Amy Norris
Illustrated by
Alexis Olguin & Amy Norris

© 2017 Amy Norris
Reservation of Rights
ISBN-9780692926390

TBT Ministries NPO
www.trainupachildministries.com
www.truthbetoldministries.com